101

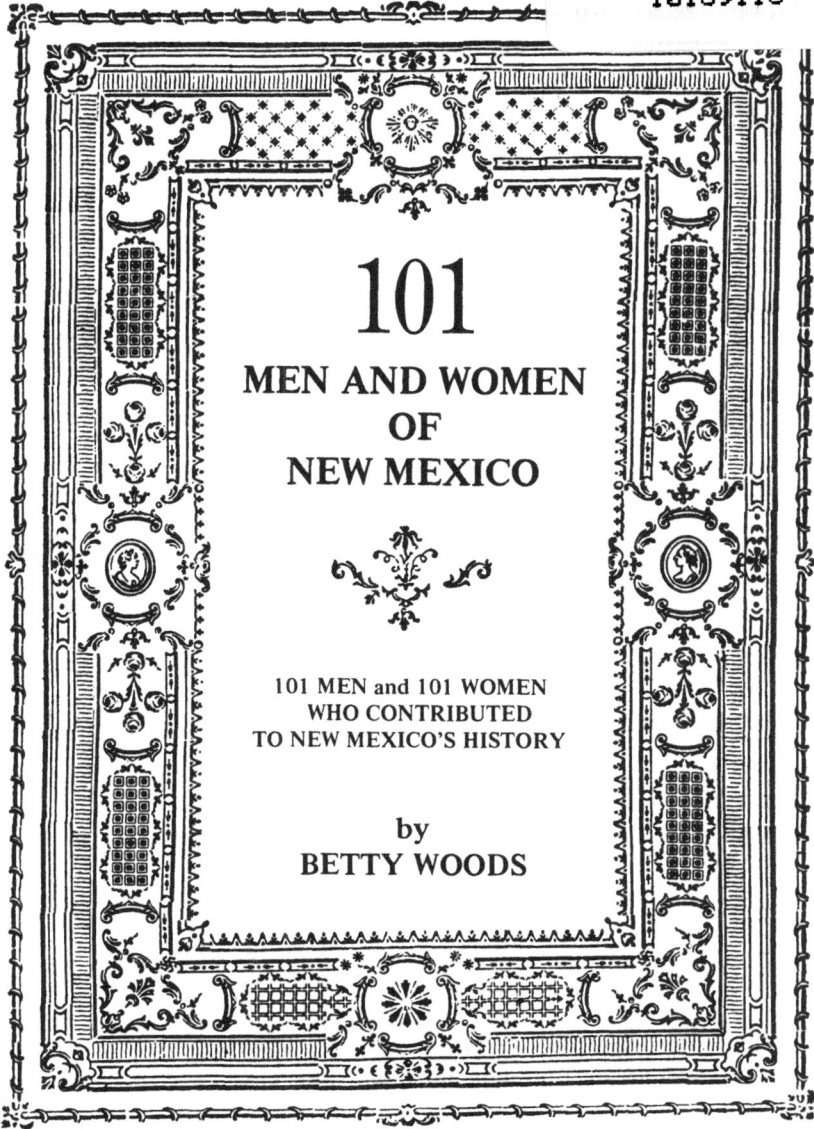

MEN AND WOMEN
OF
NEW MEXICO

101 MEN and 101 WOMEN
WHO CONTRIBUTED
TO NEW MEXICO'S HISTORY

by
BETTY WOODS

THE SUNSTONE PRESS
Santa Fe, New Mexico

To the Men & Women of New Mexico who made history.

PREFACE

These 101 men and 101 women who made history in New Mexico are people of adventure and challengers of destiny. The early ones explored and pioneered in this land of paradox. Today's are meeting successfully the highly complex problems and prejudices of the contemporary world.

Between the years of Fray Marcos de Niza and the Moon Men is a vast pageant of history played by the men and women appearing in this book. With rocket speed we span the centuries from 1536 to astronauts Edgar Mitchell and Harrison Schmidt as they fly to the moon.

The purpose of this little book is to acquaint you quickly with those men and women whose accomplishments left a deep imprint on our state. To a great extent New Mexico is what it is today for their having been here. You'll find their names chiselled on cliffsides, in ancient ruins, in journals and in modern news media. And you will meet for the first time some humble people whose stories have never been recognized before. All these people, the known and unknown, in their very special experiences merit your acquaintance.

Betty Woods

101 MEN OF NEW MEXICO

1. **ABERT, Lt. J. W.** (1820–1897)
   Mapped much of New Mexico in 1846–47 for U.S. Government. A keen observer, he kept a full, accurate diary, describing the territory in vivid words, with water color illustrations.
2. **ANDERSON, Clinton Presba** (1895–1975)
   Constantly in public office from 1941 to 1973, as Congressman, U.S. Senator, Secretary of Agriculture and War Food Administrator under President Truman. Fostered Clinton P. Anderson Room at University of New Mexico Library for preserving Western Frontier History.
3. **ARMIJO, Gov. Manuel** (1790–1853)
   Last governor of New Mexico under Mexican rule. A notorious, ambitious man. Fled before Kearney's army in 1846 without offering effective resistance.
4. **BACA, Elfego** (1865–1945)
   Colorful Albuquerque lawyer and politico. In 1884 he successfully withstood prolonged attack by 80 cowboys at Reserve, N.M. Created legend he couldn't be killed. Acquitted four times of murder.
5. **BANCROFT, Hubert Howe** (1832–1918)
   Famous historian. His works included history of New Mexico and Arizona, covering period of 1530–1888.
6. **BANDELIER, Adolph F.** (1849–1914)
   Swiss-American scientist and writer. Wrote history of New Mexico, period 1880–1886. Bandelier National Monument named for this archaeologist and historian of the Southwest.
7. **BEAUBIEN, Charles** (About 1800–1864)
   Part owner of far–flung Maxwell Land Grant. His daughter Luz married Lucien Maxwell. Prominent as banker, businessman.
8. **BECKNELL, William** (1790–1832)
   As fur trader brought first wagons over Santa Fe Trail in 1822. Has been called Father of Santa Fe Trail.
9. **BENT, Charles** (1799–1847)
   First civil governor of New Mexico under American rule. One of three brothers who built and operated Bent's Fort. Killed at Taos in Mexican-Indian uprising.
10. **BILLY THE KID (William Bonney)** (1859–1881)
    Notorious Western outlaw. Killed by Sheriff Pat Garrett at Fort Sumner, N.M.
11. **BLUMENSCHEIN, Ernest** (1874–1960)
    Co-founder, with Bert Phillips and others, of the important Taos Art Colony. Won renown as painter of New Mexico Indians and landscapes.

12. **BOLACK, Tom** (1919–   )
Self-made millionaire oil man. His strong social consciousness prompts vast efforts in land and wild game conservation. Lt. Governor and Governor of New Mexico 1961–1963. Home, Farmington, N.M.

13. **BYNNER, Harold Witter** (1881–1968)
World renowned poet and man of letters. Many years a resident of Santa Fe.

14. **CARLTON, Brigadier General James** (1814–1873)
Led the California Column to New Mexico in 1861. Directed roundup of Navajo Indians by Kit Carson, for internment at Bosque Redondo.

15. **CARSON, Kit** (1809–1869)
Great scout, soldier and frontiersman. At age 16 escaped from Missouri apprenticeship, joined Bent's Santa Fe caravan and began fabulous life. Saddlemaker to whom Kit was bound offered one cent reward for him.

16. **CASSIDY, Butch** (1865–1906)
Outlaw gang leader, known also as George Leroy Parker. Once owned a saloon at Alma, N.M. His Butch Cassidy gang operated extensively over Southwest.

17. **CASSIDY, Gerald** (1879–1934)
Ranked with Phillips and Blumenschein as original founders of Taos Art Colony. His paintings of New Mexico scenes and Indian subjects are in famous collections the world over. He used the Zia sun symbol as part of his professional name.

18. **CASTAÑO DE SOSA, Gaspar** (Birth and death dates not recorded)
In 1590 he made the first attempt to colonize New Mexico. His tragic failure helped to guide Oñate to success with his colony seven years later. His *Journal* is a valuable historical document.

19. **CATRON, Tom** (1840–1921)
U.S. Senator, lawyer, practical politician. Won renown as a trial lawyer. District judge southwest New Mexico. Catron County named for him.

20. **CHAVEZ, Dennis** (1888-1962)
U.S. Senator from New Mexico for over 30 years. Generally supported liberal political movements of his period. Home, Albuquerque.

21. **CHISUM, John** (1824–1884)
Trail herder who became cattle king of New Mexico in Pecos Valley.

22. **CHIVINGTON, Col. John M.** (1821–1894)
Commanded Colorado Volunteers at Glorieta Pass battle in 1862, contributing to defeat of the Confederates. Not long thereafter discredited by his massacre of Indians at Sand Creek.

23. **COCHISE** (Date of birth unknown. Died 1874)
As chief of Chiricahua Apaches became one of the great Apache leaders. Was prodded into war against whites by misjudgment of young Lt. Bascom. Has been portrayed in several movies.

24. **COE, George**   (1856–1941)

A participant in Lincoln County War. Rancher and citizen of prominence in later years. Town of Glencoe named for Coe family.

25. **COOKE, Capt. Phillip St. George**   (1809–1895)

Commanded U.S. Dragoons, led Mormon Batallion to California during war with Mexico. Explored Southwest for wagon routes to California.

26. **CORONADO, Francisco Vasquez de**   (1510–1554)

Led big exploration party to New Mexico 1539–41. Reached many New Mexico pueblos. Seized pueblo near Bernalillo for use as headquarters. Explored as far east as Kansas.

27. **CURRY, George**   (1861–1947)

Territorial governor of New Mexico in 1907. Defeated Elfego Baca for Congress 1911. Three times erroneously reported dead. Led exciting life as soldier, adventurer, lawyer and politician. Curry County named for him.

28. **DAVIS, W. W. H.**   (1820–1910)

U.S. Territorial Attorney for New Mexico. Acting governor of Territory 1855. Author of *El Gringo,* a highly valuable study of life in New Mexico in 1850's.

29. **DE ANZA, Juan Bautista**   (1725–1788)

Indefatigable explorer of American Southwest. Governor of New Mexico in late 1770's. Established a route to Pacific and settled San Francisco. Campaigned against Comanche Indians and other hostiles.

30. **DE BACA, Cabeza**   (No records of birth and death)

Spanish explorer shipwrecked on Texas Coast. With few followers wandered across continent to Spanish settlements on Gulf of California—a truly great saga.

31. **DE NIZA, Fray Marcos**

(Date of birth unknown. Died in Mexico City 1558)

Priest-explorer who wrote extensively of what he saw at Zuni and other places at time of Coronado.

32. **DE VARGAS, Gen. Don Diego**

(Birth unrecorded. Died 1704 at Bernalillo.)

In 1692 reconquered New Mexico after Pueblo Indian revolt of 1680. Recolonized New Mexico with 70 families, a retinue of 100 soldiers, and Franciscan priests and aides.

33. **DONIPHON, Col. Alexander**   (1808–1887)

Led 1100 Americans against Mexico, via El Paso, in 1846–47. Defeated Mexican army near El Paso and again at Sacramento near Chihuahua City. Conducted foray against Navajos, effecting treaty at Bear Springs (Fort Wingate).

34. **DORSEY, Stephen W.**   (1842–1916)

Rags to riches U.S. Senator. Built unique mansion, still standing, southeast of Raton. In mail route scandal the celebrated Robert Ingersoll defended Dorsey, gaining his acquittal.

35. **EDDY, Charles D.**   (1857–1931)

As empire builder he promoted land developments, railroads, cattle interests in eastern New Mexico. Eddy County bears his name.

36. **EMORY, Lt. W. H.** (1811–1887)

Author of *Notes of a Military Reconnaissance,* a tremendously important report on the then little-known Southwest. He married the great-granddaughter of Benjamin Franklin.

37. **ESTEVAN (var. Estaban)** (Birth date unrecorded. Killed 1539 or 1540)

Once a Negro slave of Arabs, he was shipwrecked with DeBaca. Colorful, arrogant, he crossed New Mexico in a fabulous achievement. Zuni Indians killed him for wanton transgressions.

38. **FALL, A. B.** (1861–1944)

U.S. Senator and Secretary of Interior under President Harding. Had important cattle holdings at Three Rivers, N.M. Central figure in Teapot Dome scandal, which resulted in his sentence to New Mexico State prison at Santa Fe.

39. **FERGUSSON, Harvey** (1890–1971)

Author of Southwest books of importance. First realistic novel of contemporary New Mexico, *Blood of the Conquerors,* 1921.

40. **FITZPATRICK, George** (1904–   )

Editor of *New Mexico Magazine* for many years. Author of several prestigious books on the Southwest. Home, Albuquerque.

41. **FOSTER, Bobby** (1938–   )

World Champion light heavyweight from 1968 until retiring undefeated in 1974. Successfully defended title 14 times. Only world prizefight champion from New Mexico. Now a sergeant in Bernalillo County Sheriff's department. Home, Albuquerque.

42. **FOUNTAIN, Judge Albert J.** (1838–1896)

After prosecuting cattle rustlers at Lincoln, he with 12-year-old son mysteriously disappeared in vicinity of San Augustine Pass, supposedly murdered.

43. **GARRETT, Pat** (1850–1908)

Sheriff made famous by his killing of Billy the Kid at Fort Sumner, July 14, 1881.

44. **GERONIMO** (Birth unrecorded. Died 1909 at Fort Sill)

Most vengeful Apache raider in the Southwest. With a handful of warriors pitted against several thousand white troops, he demonstrated rare military prowess. Final surrender 1885 at Skeleton Canyon. Imprisoned in Florida and Fort Sill, Okla.

45. **GODDARD, Robert Hutchings** (1882–1945)

Father of rocketry and a space pioneer. Experimented with rockets in his home town of Roswell.

46. **GOODNIGHT, Charles B.** (1836–1929)

Celebrated cattleman and founder of cattle trails. The Goodnight–Loving Trail led from Texas into New Mexico and northward.

47. **GREGG, Josiah** (1806–1850)

Trader on Santa Fe and Chihuahua Trails. Author of the highly important book *Commerce of the Prairies.*

48. **HAGERMAN, James John** (1839–1909)

Eastern New Mexico empire builder. Promoter of extensive irrigation projects and land developments. His many enterprises included banking.

49. **HEWETT, Edgar Lee, Ph.D.**   (1865–1946)
     Leading archaeologist in New Mexico. His extensive writings on New Mexico archaeology and Indian arts are considered authoritative.

50. **HILTON, Conrad**   (1887–   )
     Founder and owner of vast international hotel chain. His one check for $7,500,000 paid for Palmer House, Chicago. New Mexico legislator following statehood. His philanthropy supports many social endeavors. Born at San Antonio, N.M.

51. **HODGE, Frederick Webb, Ph.D.**   (1864–1956)
     Archaeologist of the Museum of the American Indian. Best known work, *Spanish Explorers in Southwest, U.S.* Did many translations Spanish to English.

52. **HORGAN, Paul**   (1904–   )
     Writer-historian. *Great Rivers,* featuring Rio Grande, is probably his most notable work. It won Guggenheim Award in 1947.

53. **HURD, Peter**   (1904–   )
     A leading contemporary artist of New Mexico. Owns a going ranch at San Patricio, N.M. Painted the controversial portrait of Lyndon B. Johnson. Wife is Henrietta Wyeth Hurd, a well-known portrait painter.

54. **KEARNY, Gen. Stephen Watts**   (1794–1848)
     Headed American forces into New Mexico in 1846, gaining possession of the territory without a major battle. Author of the Kearny Code.

55. **KELEHER, William**   (1886–1972)
     Early-day lawyer. Historian of note, specializing in New Mexico and Southwest history and biography. Albuquerque, home.

56. **KETCHUM, Black Jack**   (1865 or '66–1901)
     Outlaw and train robber. Hanged in Clayton, N.M.

57. **LA FARGE, Oliver**   (1901–1963)
     Prolific writer, usually using Southwest background. Won Pulitzer prize in 1929 with *Laughing Boy,* a novel with Navajo background. Santa Fe was his part-time home.

58. **LAMY, Bishop John B.**   (1818–1888)
     Instituted Catholic church reforms. Established first English-speaking school in New Mexico Territory 1851. His life inspired Willa Cather's novel, *Death Comes for the Archbishop.*

59. **LAWRENCE, D. H.**   (1885–1930)
     Controversial author whose ranch home and grave near Taos currently is a prestigious spot. Wrote *Women in Love.*

60. **LEE, Oliver**   (1865–1941)
     Oldtime cowman, owning Dog Canyon Ranch. Involved in Lincoln County War. Member State Senate. Led a colorful, eventful life.

61. **LILLY, Ben**   (1856–1936)
     Renowned bear and mountain lion hunter. Employed in hunting parties of Theodore Roosevelt and millionaires. Lived a primitive life, scorning beds and roof. Had home base on GOS Ranch, Grant County, New Mexico, for twenty years.

62. **LOVING, Oliver**   (1836–1867)
    With Charles Goodnight blazed 2000-mile cattle trail from Texas
to Wyoming. Died at Fort Stanton from wound inflicted by Comanche
Indians two months before.

63. **LUMMIS, Charles**   (1859–1928)
    Among first to write about New Mexico and its people, separate
from cowboy life. His fame was established by his book *Land of Poco
Tiempo*.

64. **MAGOFFIN, Samuel**   (1800–1888)
    Trader on Santa Fe Trail and Chihuahua Trail when General
Kearny marched into New Mexico. Going ahead of Kearny, Magoffin
influenced Governor Armijo to abandon the Territory's defense. Wife
Susan kept the famous diary.

65. **MANGUS, Colorado**   (Birth unrecorded–1863)
    Strong Chiricahua Apache chief often friendly to whites. Killed
by U.S. soldiers at Apache Tejo (near present Hurley) under questionable
circumstances.

66. **MARCY, Capt. R. B.**   (1812–1887)
    Surveyed and mapped a better Santa Fe Trail as Army engineer
following U.S. acquisition of New Mexico. Fort Marcy, overlooking city
of Santa Fe, was named for him.

67. **MARTINEZ, Paddy**   (1888–1969)
    Navajo who discovered uranium in Ambrosia Lake area, start-
ing most extensive explorations and development in all uranium history.
Spent his later years in Santa Fe.

68. **MAULDIN, Bill**   (1921–   )
    His humorous "Up Front" cartoons of World War II won a
Pulitzer Prize. Later he became a writer and newspaper correspondent,
covering world-wide assignments. He has written several books with
political slant. Resides in Santa Fe and Chicago.

69. **MAXWELL, Lucien**   (1818–1875)
    Owner of vast, much-contested Maxwell Land Grant of
1,714,000 acres. Lived magnificently and magnanimously in affluent
years. Had heavy involvements in banking, mining and trading posts.

70. **McCOMAS, Judge H. C.**   (–1883)
    Killed by Apache raiders under Chatto at Gold Gulch near
Silver City in 1883. Mrs. McComas was slain there also. Their small son
Charles was carried off, never to be found.

71. **McJUNKIN, George**   (1856–1922)
    Negro cowboy credited with discovering New World's first ac-
cepted Paleo-Indian site near Folsom, N.M. This early Indian hunter, the
Folsom Man, dates back to about 8000 B.C.

72. **MERIWETHER, Gov. David**   (1800–1892)
    As an adventurous young trader he was imprisoned at Santa Fe
in 1819 after Mexicans captured him in a band of raiding Pawnee Indians.
After 34 years he returned as appointed governor of the Territory, serving
1853–1857.

73. **MITCHELL, Navy Commander Edgar D.**   (1930–   )
     First man from New Mexico to set foot on the moon. Was pilot of lunar nodule Apollo 14, January 1971. With Allen Sheppard gathered priceless lunar specimens. Home town is Artesia.

74. **MOMADAY, Al**   (1913–   )
     Kiowa Indian artist whose paintings hang in Gilcrease Institute, Tulsa and in other celebrated collections. Is father of N. Scott Momaday. Husband of Natachee, writer and artist. Jemez Springs, N.M., home.

75. **MOMADAY, N. Scott, Ph.D.**   (1934–   )
     Kiowa Indian writer, poet, lecturer. Author of 1969 Pulitzer Prize winner, *House Made of Dawn*. Jemez Springs, N.M. and California, his homes.

76. **OÑATE, Juan de**   (1549–1624)
     Established first Spanish colony in New Mexico, at San Juan, August 18, 1598.

77. **OTERO, Gov. Miguel A.**   (1859–1944)
     Held longest territorial governorship, 1897–1906. Wrote *My Life on the Frontier* and *My Nine Years as Governor of the Territory of New Mexico*. Otero County named for him.

78. **PERSHING, Gen. John J.**   (1860–1948)
     Commanded U.S. Expeditionary Forces of World War I in France. Led pursuit of Pancho Villa after Columbus raid. He was a second lieutenant at Fort Bayard for a brief time during Apache trouble.

79. **PHILLIPS, Bert Greer**   (1868–1956)
     With other noted artists established the Taos Art Colony. His most famous painting is probably "The Moonlight Forest Song." Phillips' works are owned by many world art centers.

80. **POPÉ**   (–1688)
     San Juan Pueblo medicine man who led the successful rebellion against Spanish rule in 1680.

81. **PYLE, Ernie**   (1900–1943)
     Great World War II reporter. Wrote *Brave Men* and *This Is Your War*. Killed by Japanese sniper's bullet in South Pacific. His home in Albuquerque houses Ernie Pyle Branch Library.

82. **RHODES, Eugene Manlove**   (1869–1934)
     With a background of early cowboy life in Sierra County, he became one of the most widely acclaimed Western writers. *Saturday Evening Post* ran many of his novels serially.

83. **RUXTON, George Frederick**   (1821–1848)
     A young English vagabond, he wrote two American classics about his experiences in the early wild West, *Life in the Far West* and *Ruxton of the Rockies*. Much of these deals with New Mexico.

84. **SANCHEZ, Robert Fortune**   (1934–   )
     Tenth Archbishop of the Diocese of Santa Fe. He is the first Spanish-American Archbishop and the youngest in the United States. Santa Fe, home.

85. **SANDOVAL, Antonio**   (Birth and death unrecorded)
     Leading Navajo slave raider in 1850's. Raided Navajo and other reservations. Sold captives in Abiquiu and Cebolleta slave markets.

86. **SCHMIDT, Harrison, Ph.D.** (1936–   )
Apollo 17 astronaut. First civilian scientist going into outer space. On moon trip 1972. Silver City and Hurley claim him.

87. **SHARP, Joseph Henry** (1859–1953)
Another of those great artists who originated the Taos Art Colony. His Indian life studies, typified by "Indian at Work," are world-renowned.

88. **SIBLEY, Gen. Henry** (1816–1886)
Led Confederate invasion of New Mexico in 1862. Defeated and turned back at Glorieta Pass.

89. **SLAUGHTER, John** (1841–1922)
Famous trail herder. Established Slaughter Brothers Trail across southern New Mexico. Became distinguished rancher and sheriff of southeast Arizona.

90. **ST. VRAIN, Ceran** (1802–1870)
A romantic figure. Partner of Bent Brothers. Merchant, fur trader, military man. Once owned Sangre de Cristo Grant. Died at Mora, a wealthy man. Buried with high military honors from Fort Union.

91. **THORPE, N. Howard (Jack)** (1867–1940)
Cowboy poet who put the "feel" of the rangeland in his songs and poems. Wrote *Little Joe, the Wrangler; Songs of the Cowboys;* and *Tales of the Chuck Wagon.*

92. **TWITCHELL, Ralph Emerson** (1858–1925)
Lawyer, politician, historian, lecturer. Associated with Bandelier. Helped found the Santa Fe Fiesta. Among the first in use of movies to promote New Mexico.

93. **UNSER BROTHERS, Bob and Al** (Bob born 1934. Al born 1939.)
Albuquerque's million-dollar auto racing brothers. They have won most of the big U.S. races at least once. Al was a two-time winner of the Indianapolis 500. Own a ranch near Chama, N.M. Bobby Unser won the Indianapolis 500 in 1975.

94. **VALDEZ, Phil Isadore** (1946–1967)
Vietnam War hero killed as he saved the lives of two Marines. The USS Valdez, a new Knox-class destroyer, was named in his honor when commissioned in July 1974.

95. **VICTORIO** (–1880)
Warm Springs Apache chief who became one of the most devastating raiders in New Mexico, Arizona and Mexico. Killed by Mexican troops in Chihuahua in a battle that almost exterminated his band.

96. **VILLA, Pancho** (1877–1923)
Mexican Revolutionary general, once a bandit leader. Raided Columbus, New Mexico in 1916, precipitating General Pershing's unsuccessful pursuit of him into Mexico. Columbus now has a state Park named for Villa.

97. **VILLAGRÁ, Don Gaspar Perez de** (–   )
With Onate's colonizers. Said to have worn a false nose. Wrote the first epic poem describing New Mexico. This was published in Spain in 1610.

98. **WALLACE, General Lew** (1827–1905)

Territorial governor of New Mexico, after Civil War service in Union army as general. Carried out Washington order to end Lincoln County War. Wrote part of *Ben Hur* in old Governor's Palace, Santa Fe.

99. **WATERS, Frank** (1902-   )

Well known current writer who uses Indian and unusual western themes. Authored *The Man Who Killed the Deer* and *Masked Gods*.

100. **WILLIAMS, Old Bill** (–1849)

Eccentric Mountain Man, guide, scout, trapper, Indian trader in the Taos region and elsewhere. Although he had a Ute wife, he was killed in a skirmish with Utes.

101. **WOOTON, "Uncle" Dick** (1816–1893)

Freighter, trapper, hunter. Built toll road over Raton Pass, 1866. He fought the coming of the railroad because it hurt his toll road business.

101 WOMEN OF NEW MEXICO

1. **ABREU, Margaret** (–)
   Author, educator. Recently state comptroller. Author of *Food of the Conquerors*.

2. **AMAYA de MIGUEL, Casilda** (–)
   Thought to be the first white woman to enter New Mexico. In the 1500's she accompanied her husband, Sanchez Miguel, on the Espejo expedition.

3. **ANGEL, Paula** (–1861)
   The only woman legally hanged in New Mexico, in Las Vegas April 26, 1861, at her own expense, for the murder of her lover.

4. **ARMSTRONG, Ruth** (–)
   Author and motion picture coordinator. Through her efforts many TV and movie companies have used New Mexico locations in the 1970's. Home, Corrales, New Mexico.

5. **AUSTIN, Mary** (1868–1934)
   Distinguished author who in her many books often portrayed the enchantment of New Mexico. *Starry Adventure* is her best-known novel. Home, Santa Fe.

6. **BARCELA, Dona Gertrudis (La Tules)** (Early 1800's–1852)
   Colorful gambling woman of Santa Fe, friend of Governor Armijo and American officers.

7. **BARKER, Ruth Laughlin** (1889–1962)
   Wrote extensively of Indians and other New Mexico people. Her widely acclaimed *Caballeros* depicts her growing-up years in Santa Fe.

8. **BARTLETT, Florence** (1882–1964)
   Wealthy Chicago patroness of the arts. Built and donated to the State the Museum of International Folk Art in Santa Fe.

9. **BEAUBIEN, Luz** (1828–)
   Daughter of Carlos Beaubien. Married Lucien Maxwell at age 14 in 1842. This marriage led to the creation of the great Maxwell Land Grant empire.

10. **BENT, Mrs. Charles** (–)
    Before marriage she was Ignacia Jaramillo, one of two beautiful Jaramillo sisters. She witnessed the tragic slaying of her husband, territorial governor of New Mexico, during the Taos uprising in 1848.

11. **BENT, Mrs. William** (–)
    Cheyenne Indian woman called Owl Woman, married celebrated trader in 1837. After her death, Bent married her sister, Yellow Woman, in the late 1840's.

16

12. **BLUMENSCHEIN, Mary Green** (1868–1958)
Wife of painter Ernest Blumenschein of Taos. She did silver work in the new Mexico tradition and was an illustrator.

13. **BOYD, E., Ph.D.** (1903–1974)
Authority on santos and early New Mexico art. Renowned scholar and researcher. Curator emeritus of Spanish colonial arts for Museum of New Mexico. Santa Fe her home.

14. **BRETT, Lady Dorothy Eugenia** (1883–)
Artist of the D. H. Lawrence period of Taos. Author of *Lawrence and Brett*. Her best known painting is The Turtle Dance. Taos her home.

15. **BREWER, Madame Rebecca** (–)
In early 1900's this clever Black woman won local distinction as a *curandera* in Silver City, often using native herb medicines and concoctions. She also told fortunes and sold love potions.

16. **BULLOCK, Alice** (–)
Indefatigable Santa Fe reporter, writer, book reviewer and book editor for the *Santa Fe New Mexican. Mountain Villages* is her latest book.

17. **CARSON, Josefa** (Born about 1828)
Wife of Kit Carson, second of the Jaramillo sisters noted for their haughty, heartbreaking beauty. Married Carson in Taos in 1843.

18. **CASSIDY, Ina Sizer** (1869–1965)
Wife of master artist Gerald Cassidy of Taos. For years she wrote the feature *Arts and Artists of New Mexico* for *New Mexico Magazine*. Was a strong advocate for the preservation of New Mexico culture.

19. **CATHER, Willa** (1876–1947)
Won fame as the author of *Death Comes for the Archbishop*. A prolific writer. High in her successes was *Shadows on the Rock*. Won Pulitzer Prize in 1922 for *One of Ours*.

20. **CHACON, Mrs. Soledad** (–)
First woman to act as governor of New Mexico. As secretary of State in 1924 she became acting governor when the governor left the state temporarily.

21. **CHEROKEE DORA** (–)
Beautiful quarter-blood Cherokee who in her early twenties became an outlaw. She included robberies in her career. She killed her lover named Poker Paul. She was known also as Dora Chiquita and La Chiquita. Santa Rosa was her base of operation, around 1900.

22. **CHRISTY, Dr. Meta** (–)
First Black woman osteopath in the world. As a young doctor, she began practice in Las Vegas in the early 1900's and continued there for a lifetime of noteworthy service. Was daughter of slave parents.

23. **CHURCH, Peggy Pond** (1908–)
Author of *House at Otowi Bridge* and *The Burro of Angelitos*.

24. **CLARK, Ann Nolan** (1898–)
Prolific contemporary writer whose leading books are *In My Mother's House, Medicine Man's Daughter*, and *Along Sandy Trails*. She has published many magazine articles and stories for children.

25. **CLAYTON, Jan** (-)

Tularosa born star of TV series *Lassie* and *Nakia*. She has other stage and movie successes. Family gardens attract during Rose Festival in June.

26. **CLEAVELAND, Agnes Morley** (1874–1938)

Author of *No Life for a Lady*, a Houghton-Mifflin prize-winning fact book.

27. **COE, Louise** (-)

First woman member of New Mexico State Senate, 1925. Strong advocate of higher educational standards. Member of the pioneer Coe family of Lincoln County. Town of Glencoe named for her family.

28. **DUTTON, Dr. Bertha** (1903–)

Anthropologist, archaeologist. Former research director and curator at the Museum of Navajo Ceremonial Art, Santa Fe. Has supervised important archaeological "digs" at numerous world sites.

29. **DYSART, Stella** (1878–1966)

Best-known woman "wildcatter" and only woman to strike it big in uranium. Achieved great wealth in uranium mines in Ambrosia Lake area. Home was Albuquerque.

30. **ELLISON, Virginia** (-)

She and her husband have done a monumental job of excavating Indian ruins called Kwilleyckia on Gila River near Cliff, N.M.

31. **FERGUSSON, Erna** (1888–1964)

New Mexico's first lady of letters. Wrote *Dancing Gods* and many other books. Erna Fergusson Branch Library in Albuquerque honors her memory.

32. **FINDLEY, Grandma** (-)

La Luz pioneer woman who made her own smallpox vaccine and used it to save many lives in her community during an epidemic in the 1890's.

33. **FITZPATRICK, Mildred, Ph.D.** (-)

Educator, writer. Received the 1975 State Board of Education Award of Excellence. Governor Apodaca proclaimed June 27 Mildred Fitzpatrick Day in New Mexico. Home, Albuquerque. Wife of George Fitzpatrick, author and editor.

34. **FRISBIE, Dr. Evelyn** (1873–1965)

In 1923 established hospital in Albuquerque specializing in obstetrics, diseases of children, and gynecology. Home, Albuquerque.

35. **GAMBLIN, Becky** (-)

For a generation has directed the young people of the Methodist Church choir at Silver City in a Christmas program which each year attains magnificent proportions.

36. **GARRETT, Elizabeth** (1884–1947)

Blind daughter of Lincoln County sheriff Pat Garrett. She composed several songs, the best known being New Mexico's state song, *Fair New Mexico*. She enjoyed a friendship with Helen Keller.

37. **GARSON, Greer** (1912–)

World-famous movie star, co-owner (with husband, Col. E. E. Fogelson) of Forked Lightning Ranch northeast of Santa Fe. Benefactress of Santa Fe's Greer Garson Theater.

38. **GILPIN, Laura**   (1891–   )
   Celebrated woman photographer who specializes in studies of New Mexico scene. Her pictures have won many prestigious awards. Her book, *Enduring Navajo,* is a classic in photojournalism.

39. **GONZALES, Christine**   (–   )
   First woman locomotive engineer of the Santa Fe Railway. Third generation of a railroad family. Her grandmother was a "Harvey Girl." Her first job as engineer was dumping ore cars at the Hurley smelter.

40. **HARDIN, Helen**   (1943–   )
   Distinguished Santa Clara Indian artist. Daughter of famous Indian artist Pablita Velarde.

41. **HARWOOD, Emily**   (–   )
   Early-day Methodist missionary. In 1869 came with husband Rev. Thomas Harwood to work among the Spanish-speaking girls in New Mexico. Established Harwood School and Home for girls in Albuquerque.

42. **HAURY, Winona Margery**   (–   )
   A Navajo girl, she was the first Miss Indian America from New Mexico, 1969–70. Also, University of New Mexico Homecoming Queen 1972.

43. **HAYDEN, Mother Magdalen**   (1813–1894)
   In 1852 she led Sisters of Loretto on a three-month journey across Indian country to establish a school in Santa Fe. She later opened convents and schools in other towns in New Mexico.

44. **HERRERA, Julia**   (–   )
   First Pueblo Indian woman to become principal of a public school in New Mexico. Appointed to office in 1974 at Santo Domingo Pueblo. Harvard graduate of 1972. Home, Old Laguna Pueblo.

45. **HOLMES, Julia**   (1838–   )
   First woman to climb Pike's Peak (1858) wearing her much-publicized bloomer costume. On the summit she read aloud selections from Emerson's *Essays.* Her husband was Territorial Secretary of New Mexico.

46. **HOZES de Sanchez, Francisca**   (–   )
   Wife of Alonzo Sanchez, soldier. With husband she went the entire route on Coronado's expedition in 1540. Later she charged that Coronado prevented her and others from establishing a colony.

47. **JENKINS, Myra Ellen, Dr.**   (1916–   )
   Eminent archivist, researcher and historian of New Mexico. Current chief of the Historial Services Division in the State Records Center and Archives. Home, Santa Fe.

48. **KELEHER, Julia**   (–   )
   Writer and educator. Member of renowned pioneer family. Wrote *The Padre of Isleta,* published 1940.

49. **KING, Sissy**   (1947–   )
   This Albuquerque girl leaped to stardom in America's big-time dance team of "Bobby and Sissy" on the Lawrence Welk show.

50. **LANE, Lydia**   (–   )
Author of *I Married a Soldier* in which she describes the hardships of an army wife in early days of New Mexico. In 1861 at Fort Fillmore for a brief time, she became the only woman commanding officer in New Mexico Territory.

51. **LARGO, Marquita**   (–   )
In 1974 became first woman commissioned police officer on Navajo Indian Reservation. She was commissioned by New Mexico State Police. She works with women and juveniles as public relations officer.

52. **LAWRENCE, Frieda**   (1879–1956)
Experienced a colorful life near Taos. Wrote *Not I But the Wind*. Wife of D. H. Lawrence, controversial author.

53. **LEA, Sallie Wilde**   (–   )
Cattle queen in eastern New Mexico in 1880's. Struggled for education for settlers at Roswell.

54. **LEE, Frances Marren**   (–   )
Prominent ranch holdings, west slope of San Mateo Mountains. Republican National Committee Woman. Active in educational work — from Board of Regents of the University of New Mexico to local schools.

55. **LOPEZ, Dona Teresa**   (–   )
Wife of New Mexico governor under Spain in 1659–1661. She and her husband were sent to prison in Mexico City, charged with: sleeping in separate rooms, bathing on Fridays, reading a book in Italian. Her husband died in the prison. She was liberated after six years. Wrote important documents of life in Santa Fe during the 1600's.

56. **LUHAN, Mabel Dodge**   (–   )
Author of *Lorenzo in Taos* and other books. Heiress of much of original Dodge Motor Company fortune, she married Tony Lujan, full-blood Taos Indian. She was a patroness of the Taos Art Colony.

57. **LYNCH, Mary**   (1938–   )
Founding editor of the *Jicarilla Chieftain*, first newspaper published by an Indian tribe in New Mexico. Educated at Santa Fe Indian School and Fort Lewis College, Durango. She is part Jicarilla Apache.

58. **MAGOFFIN, Susan Shelby**   (1827–1855)
Recorded an extremely valuable account of her travels with her trader husband in the far west and Mexico, particularly for New Mexico, in 1846–47.

59. **MAIN, Dorothy**   (–   )
When an unmarried teacher on the Navajo Reservation, she rescued and adopted two Navajo baby girls, reared them as her own and followed through with them in their married lives. Now retired, living in Albuquerque.

60. **MALDONADO, Maria**   (–   )
Wife of Juan de Paradines, she was one of three women accompanying husbands on Coronado's expedition of 1540–42. Helped care for sick and injured soldiers.

61. **MARIA, the Potter (Maria Martinez)**   (1881–   )
World-famous San Ildefonso Indian potter whose works are in museums all over the world.

20

62. **MARRIOTT, Alice**   (1910–   )
    Author of *The Valley Below and Maria the Potter of San Ildefonso,* among other works. Anthropologist, notably of Pueblos and Kiowa.

63. **MASSY, Louise**   (–   )
    Singer, musician, and composer of Western songs. Composed *My Adobe Hacienda.* Gained note in the long-time radio and TV performances of Louise Massey and the Westerners. She owned a ranch on Rio Hondo, west of Roswell.

64. **McMAHAN, Kathryn**   (–   )
    Librarian and contemporary Southwest researcher. Her wide knowledge of source materials and attitude of helpfulness contribute immeasurably to the work of writers and researchers. Albuquerque resident.

65. **McSWEEN, Susan (Barber)**   (–   )
    Widow of A. A. McSween of Lincoln County War fame and herself prominent in the burning of her home in Lincoln. She later became cattle queen of New Mexico, headquartered in Rock House at Three Rivers.

66. **MERA, Reba**   (–   )
    Sewed the first New Mexico state flag in 1923. Nicknamed "Mrs. Betsy Ross of New Mexico."

67. **MOMADAY, Natachee**   (–   )
    Jemez Springs writer-artist completing remarkable Momaday trio of mother, father, son. Husband Al is a distinguished painter. Son Scott is a Pulitzer Prize winner.

68. **NEFF, Francine**   (–   )
    She is the current Treasurer of the United States. Look for her name on currency (1975 and later). Albuquerque claims her.

69. **NEWCOMB, Franc**   (1887–1970)
    Wrote *Navajo Omens and Taboos, Hosteen Klah,* and *Navajo Folk Tales.* Wife of Arthur Newcomb, old-time Navajo trader.

70. **O'KEEFE, Georgia**   (1887–   )
    Termed greatest living woman painter. Her pictures of New Mexico scenes and people command highest world acclaim. Homes: Abiquiu, Santa Fe, New York City.

71. **ORCHARD, Sadie**   (–   )
    Colorful woman stagecoach driver. Owned the stages she drove from Kingston via Hillsboro to Lake Valley. Also ran a hotel in Hillsboro — all in 1880's.

72. **ORTIZ, Vernavé**   (–   )
    At age 15, the only survivor of an Apache attack on a wagon train at Burro Springs, Grant County. After mistreatment she was scalped, left for dead. A posse took her to Silver City where she lived a long life, becoming a midwife. She always wore a black cap over her scalped head.

73. **OTERO, Nina**   (–   )
    Wrote with authority on Spanish customs of New Mexico. Her book, *Old Spain in Our Southwest,* is a research classic.

74. **PARSONS, Elsie Clews** (1875–1941)

Anthropologist, ethnologist and fieldworker with the Southwest Indians. Recorded the cultural and religious aspects of their lives.

75. **PENALOSE, Dona Eufemia** (–)

Wife of a royal ensign who accompanied her husband with Onate's 130-family colonizers. In a subsequent Indian attack on San Juan Pueblo she stationed armed women on rooftops to help repel attackers in the late 1590's.

76. **POE, Sophia** (–)

Wife of Sheriff Poe. In her book, *Buckboard Days,* she writes vividly of the exciting 1880's in Lincoln County area of New Mexico.

77. **REICHARD, Gladys** (1893–1955)

Highly regarded writer on New Mexico country. Her *Spider Woman* is rated a classic of its kind. Taught Navajos to write and read their own language. Wrote Navajo grammar.

78. **RHODES, Mary D.** (–)

Wife of Eugene Manlove Rhodes, widely acclaimed western writer. Wrote *Hired Man on Horseback.*

79. **RICE, Alice, Dr.** (–)

Led efforts to establish a hospital and home for the sick in Las Vegas beginning in 1895. Perhaps she was the first woman doctor to practice medicine in New Mexico. Dr. Emma Purnell followed in 1905 in Las Vegas.

80. **ROBERT, Sallie L.** (1858– ?)

Daughter of James Chisum, niece of John Chisum, she became pioneer cattlewoman and successful business woman. Once owned site of present Artesia. Operated Halfway House in Pecos Valley and a hotel in Roswell.

81. **ROOKE, Sarah J.** (–)

Telephone operator heroine of Folsom. In 1908 when a disastrous flood was sweeping toward Folsom she stuck to her switchboard, phoning warnings, until she herself was trapped in the water and drowned.

82. **SAWYER, Dessie** (–)

Owns extensive oil and ranch interests in Eastern New Mexico. Active in many endeavors for public service. Was Democratic National Committee Woman for 24 years. Important political figure.

83. **SHEPPARD, Agnes Kelly** (–)

While he was confined at Ojo Caliente, in early 1880's, Geronimo saved baby Agnes from drowning in irrigation ditch. A typical ranch woman, with a bubbling sense of humor, she sang cowboy songs with gusto, accompanying herself on guitar.

84. **SHONNARD, Eugenie F. (Mrs. Gordon Ludlam)** (1886–)

World-acclaimed sculptress. Ranked as greatest animal figure creator. Works in bronze, stone, wood, marble, and granite. She has pieces in Luxemborg Galleries of Paris, Metropolitan Museum, New York, and in other great galleries.

85. **SISTER BLANDINA** (1850–1941)

This remarkable woman came to New Mexico as a missionary of the Sisters of Charity, a Catholic order. She established a school in Old Town Albuquerque. Her missionary work during the rugged Territorial days constitutes a beautiful saga of the Southwest.

86. **STEVENSON, Mrs. Matilda Coxe** (–)
Made the first important ethnobotanical study of Zuni Indians in 1879. Is a researcher's guide.

87. **STOCKTON, Pansy** (1895–1972)
Flamboyant artist called "Sun Painter," of Santa Fe. Used dry plant materials for unusual effects. Said to have arranged materials with her toes. Her pictures shown in Buckingham Palace, the White House, and in prominent galleries.

88. **TICHY, Dr. Marie** (1884–1975)
First woman dentist to practice in New Mexico. She practiced for 45 years at Las Vegas, N.M. Home in later days, Deming.

89. **TINGLEY, Carrie** (1877–1961)
Wife of former governor, Clyde Tingley (served 1933–37). She showed great concern for needy children. For her endeavors there, her name is perpetuated in Carrie Tingley Children's Hospital at Truth or Consequences, N.M., built in 1937.

90. **TURNER, Addie** (–)
The first woman to descend into Carlsbad Caverns. She went with her brother and Jim White. They went down in the "bucket" and explored Bat Cave in early 1900's.

91. **UNDERHILL, Ruth** (1884–)
The First Penthouse Dwellers of America was her first book success. Another book, *The Navajos,* has gone through several editions. She is regarded as an authority on Pueblo and Navajo Indians.

92. **UNSER, Mary** (–1975)
Center of famed auto racing family (husband and three sons), with two sons now the greatest winners of all time. Ma Unser every year cooks a traditional fiesta chili dinner for "Indy" racers at Indianapolis. Home, Albuquerque.

93. **VELARDE, Pablita** (1918–)
Santa Clara Indian artist who has won many awards with her paintings. Mother of Helen Hardin, also a famed painter.

94. **VESTAL, Madame** (–)
As beautiful Belle Siddons, she was a Southern spy during the Civil War. Later became a skilled blackjack dealer, then drifted into bawdy gambling houses. In early 1880's had an establishment at Las Vegas, N.M. Died in a San Francisco jail.

95. **WALLACE, Susan E.** (–)
Wife of Lew Wallace, Territorial governor. Her *Land of the Pueblos* describes New Mexico of the 1880–1890 period. Contributed to the *Atlantic Monthly* and many newspapers.

96. **WALTERS, Mary** (–)
First woman district judge in New Mexico. Appointed in 1971 by Gov. Bruce King. Home, Albuquerque.

97. **WARNER, Dr. Estella Ford** (1891–1974)
One of the nation's most honored public health officers, much of her work having been in New Mexico. The first woman commissioned a Major in Public Health Service. Won many awards in medicine. Home, Albuquerque.

98. **WAUNEKA, Dr. Annie** (1910–   )

Daughter of distinguished Navajo chief, Henry Chee Dodge. First woman member of Navajo tribal council. President Johnson gave her the Medal of Freedom in 1969 for her improvement of Navajo health.

99. **WHEELWRIGHT, Mary Cabot** (1878–1958)

Authority on Navajo rites and ceremonies. Recorded Hosteen Klah's story of Navajo creation. This and other recordings of Navajo chants are in the archives of the New Mexico Museum of Navajo Ceremonial Art.

100. **WILSON, Jane Adeline** (–   )

Captured by Comanches in 1870's. After several months of captivity she escaped alone. Spanish-speaking Comancheros found her wandering on plains near death and returned her to civilization and normal life.

101. **WYETH, Henriette (Mrs. Peter Hurd)** (1907–   )

Eminent portrait painter from the prominent Wyeth family of artists. Home, San Patricio, N.M.

Editor's Note: Dates not included were not available.